McPHERSON GOES TO WORK

John McPherson

ZondervanPublishingHouse
Grand Rapids, Michigan

A Division of HarperCollins*Publishers*

McPherson Goes to Work
Copyright © 1992 by John McPherson

Requests for information should be addressed to
Zondervan Publishing House
Grand Rapids, Michigan 49530

Library of Congress Cataloging-in-Publication Data

McPherson, John, 1959–
    McPherson goes to work / John McPherson.
      p. cm.
    ISBN 0-310-58611-9
    1. Work—Humor. 2. Offices—Humor. 3. Business—Humor. 4. Work—Carica-
tures and cartoons. 5. Office—Caricatures and cartoons. 6. Business—Caricatures and
cartoons. 7. American wit and humor.
    I. Title.
    PN6231.W644M37   1992
    741.5′973—dc20
                                     92-2832
                                       CIP

Some of these cartoons originally appeared in *Physician's Management* and *The Satur-
day Evening Post*. Many thanks to those publications for allowing us to reprint them.

Printed in the United States of America

92 93 94 95 96 97 / LP / 10 9 8 7 6 5 4 3 2 1

In memory of Peter Neal,
a master of the fine art
of laughter

Special thanks to Bob Watkins
for providing
the real-life experiences
upon which many
of these cartoons are based

Front-cover watercolor
by Laura McPherson

Back-cover photo
by Steve Robb

"I'VE GOT A LONG DAY AHEAD OF ME."

"I'LL BE THERE IN A SECOND."

ACCOUNTING MANAGER HANK CLEMMER FIRMLY BELIEVES
THAT A COMFORTABLE EMPLOYEE IS A LAZY EMPLOYEE.

"THIS DARNED THING IS JAMMED AGAIN."

HAVING NARROWED THE FIELD OF CANDIDATES TO THREE, PERSONNEL GOES THROUGH THE FINAL SELECTION PROCESS.

"PERSONALLY, I THINK THIS NEW REORGANIZATION PLAN STINKS."

AFTER THE SLIDE PROJECTOR BROKE, LLOYD'S VISUAL PRESENTATION ON 3RD QUARTER SALES TOOK A DRASTIC TURN FOR THE WORSE.

"LOOKS LIKE I NEED TO SWITCH AND START USING _THIS_ ARM TO HIT THE SNOOZE BUTTON."

"MY BLOW-DRYER IS BROKEN."

STELLA KNEW THE IMPORTANCE OF BEING DISCREET WHEN MAKING PERSONAL PHONE CALLS.

AS SOON AS SHE BEGAN TO READ THE MINUTES OF THE LAST MEETING, THE BOARD MEMBERS KNEW THAT MRS. FELSTNER WAS NOT GOING TO WORK OUT AS THE NEW SECRETARY.

"SORRY, SIR. WE'VE STILL GOT A FEW BUGS TO WORK OUT."

"READY TO _WORK_ AT 8 O'CLOCK, VELEZ! NOT JUST _HERE_ AT 8 O'CLOCK! READY TO _WORK_!

HOPEFULLY, MAINTENANCE WOULD TAKE THE HINT
AND TURN THE HEAT UP A NOTCH.

"I THINK I FOUND THE PROBLEM. WE LEFT OUT A COMMA."

VERN'S TENDENCY TO FIDGET DURING INTERVIEWS COSTS HIM ANOTHER JOB.

"AS MOST OF YOU KNOW, THE COMPANY HAS UNDERGONE SOME CUTBACKS RECENTLY."

ALTHOUGH THE NEW OFFICE CUBICLES WERE A REFRESHING CHANGE, THEY DID MAKE IT DIFFICULT TO HAVE A PRIVATE CONVERSATION.

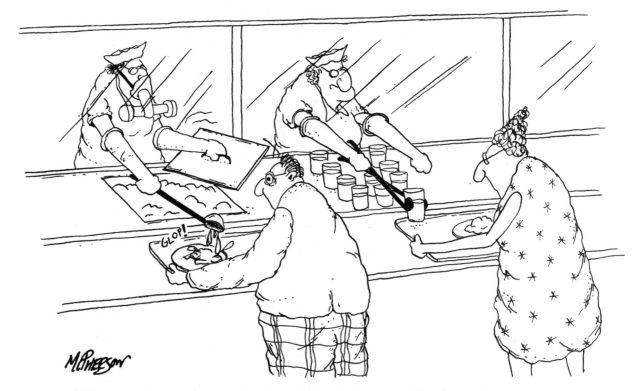

EMPLOYEES AT VALCON NUCLEAR FACILITY WERE BECOMING MORE AND MORE CONCERNED *ABOUT THE QUALITY OF THE FOOD IN THE CAFETERIA.*

MORT LASHES OUT AT THE NEW
"NO-FOOD-AT-YOUR-DESK" RULE.

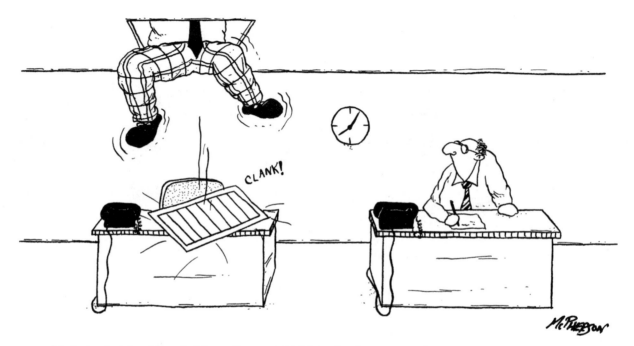

CLANK!

KNOWING HE WAS RUNNING A BIT LATE, WARREN PLAYED IT SAFE AND TOOK A ROUTE TO HIS DESK THAT WOULDN'T TAKE HIM PAST HIS BOSS'S OFFICE.

"DEE DEE VERSHAY'S DOG IS HAVING A HERNIA OPERATION. EVERYBODY'S SIGNING THIS GET-WELL CARD AND KICKING IN $10."

THE NEW COFFEE DISTRIBUTION SYSTEM NOT ONLY BOOSTED MORALE BUT ALSO CUT DOWN ON TIME SPENT MINDLESSLY LINGERING AROUND THE COFFEE MACHINE.

"YOU RODE YOUR BIKE TO WORK AGAIN, DIDN'T YOU?"

"I HAD IT INSTALLED BY AN OUTFIT CALLED _BUDGET CAR PHONES_."

REST ROOM USAGE			
EMPLOYEE	TRIPS TODAY	MONTHLY TOTAL	AVG. LENGTH OF STAY
CLARK	3	47	2 min.
FRAWLEY	6	52	4.6 min.
PATERSON	2	29	3.1 min.
MORRISON	0	4	.2 min.
MIELKE	19	33	12 min.
ROBB	13	102	34 min.
LEONARD	9	73	17 min.

MANAGEMENT FELT THAT THE NEW CHART WAS HELPFUL IN DETECTING EMPLOYEES WHO WERE ABUSING THE SYSTEM.

"MS. MORTLESON, TAKE A MEMO: ALL EMPLOYEES ARE REMINDED THAT EMPTY SODA CANS SHOULD BE RETURNED FOR DEPOSIT ON A DAILY BASIS."

"MAYBE YOU HAVEN'T HEARD, KARL, BUT IT'S SORT OF A TRADITION AROUND HERE THAT WHOEVER WINS THE 50 BUCKS IN THE SUPERBOWL POOL TAKES THE REST OF THE OFFICE OUT TO LUNCH."

THUS FAR, FRANK WASN'T TOO IMPRESSED
WITH THE COMPANY'S DENTAL PLAN.

"CHECK THE OIL, PLEASE."

STAN EXPRESSES HIS OPINION REGARDING THE NEW PIPED-IN ELEVATOR MUSIC.

"I DEMANDED THAT I BE GIVEN AN OFFICE WITH A WINDOW."

EARLY MANAGEMENT TECHNIQUES.

BOB WOULD GO TO ANY LENGTH TO GET THAT PROMOTION.

"HE DRANK THE LAST CUP OF COFFEE AND DIDN'T MAKE A FRESH POT."

"BE SURE TO COMPLIMENT HIM ON HIS WIFE AND KIDS."

· COMPANY PICNIC SIGN-UP SHEET ·
PLEASE BRING A DISH TO PASS!

NAME	DISH TO PASS
ZWEIFFEL	CHIPS
McLure	Chips
SCHMIDT	CHIPS
Johnson	Soda
Campbell	Chips
PATERSON	CHIPS
WAZNIK	CHIPS
Lusk	Soda
Gentile	Seven-Bean Salad
WHITE	CHIPS
Ballas	Chips
MATTONE	CHIPS
Ruediger	Chips
NEAL	CHIPS
Collymore	Soda
COMSTOCK	CHIPS
HUNTLEY	CHIPS

McPHERSON

"THE HEIGHT ADJUSTMENT ON THESE NEW CHAIRS IS SORT OF FINICKY, ISN'T IT?"

"WHEN WE'VE BEEN WITH THE COMPANY FOR TEN YEARS, WE GET TO PARK IN SECTION Q."

"HERE'S ONE THAT SAYS 'DON BECK' ON IT! DON BECK HASN'T WORKED HERE SINCE 1986!"

PARKING
$2 PER HOUR

"GET THE RED BUICK IN THE THIRD ROW."

"FOR CRYIN' OUT LOUD! WOULD YOU JUST TAKE A A SICK DAY FOR ONCE IN YOUR LIFE!"

"THOSE LAP-TOP COMPUTERS COST A FORTUNE."

MANAGEMENT TRAINEE J.K. BOODLEY TESTS THE
BOUNDARIES OF THE COMPANY'S NEW DRESS CODE.

"IT'S PART OF THE COMPANY'S NEW EMPHASIS ON HEALTH AND FITNESS."

"SORRY, SIR."

BLAT!

"IN THE FUTURE, I WOULD APPRECIATE A LITTLE ADVANCE NOTICE WHEN YOU BRING YOUR BOSS HOME FOR DINNER."

"IT'S MR. SIMPKINS FROM OUR CHICAGO OFFICE! HE MUST HAVE PHONED OUR FAX NUMBER BY MISTAKE!"

"IT SAYS ON YOUR RESUMÉ THAT YOU CAN TYPE 260 WORDS PER MINUTE. NO OFFENSE, MRS. BALLAS, BUT I FIND THAT PRETTY HARD TO BELIEVE."

THE DOWNSIDE OF CARPOOLING.

"YOU'LL HAVE TO BEAR WITH ME HERE. WE'RE HAVING SOME TECHNICAL DIFFICULTIES WITH OUR OVERHEAD PROJECTOR."

"SORRY ABOUT THE MIX-UP WITH THE KEYBOARDS. WE HOPE THIS WON'T AFFECT YOUR PROGRAMMING ABILITIES."

THOUGH SHE HADN'T READ IT YET, LOIS HAD A STRONG SENSE OF FOREBODING ABOUT HER ANNUAL REVIEW.

"FOR THE LAST TIME, KARDAS, YOU CAN <u>NOT</u> HAVE THE DAY AFTER THANKSGIVING OFF!"

"BUT IT WASN'T ACID! THAT WAS A CUP OF COFFEE FROM THE CAFETERIA!"

WHEN IT GOT RIGHT DOWN TO IT, NOBODY HAD TIME TO
SPEND DRYING THEIR HANDS UNDER THE NEW
ELECTRIC HAND DRYER.

"COMSTOCK'S MOVING A LITTLE SLOW ON THAT DIXON PROPOSAL. GIVE HIM 75 VOLTS FOR FIVE SECONDS. WHAT THE HECK, MAKE THAT TEN SECONDS."

NEW EMPLOYEES WERE QUICK TO NOTICE THE LITTLE CLIQUES THAT EXISTED AT THE P.L. FERNLEY COMPANY.

"I'M GETTING PRETTY FED UP WITH THIS MANDATORY OVERTIME."

THOUGH ELAINE TRIED TO BE DISCREET, PEOPLE QUICKLY HOMED IN ON THE SOURCE OF THE MICROWAVE POPCORN AROMA.

"DID SOMEBODY HERE CALL UP ABOUT TOO MUCH AIR-CONDITIONING BLOWIN' ON THEIR HEAD?"

"MY BABYSITTER'S GOT THE FLU."

JULES HALM'S OFFHAND REMARK ABOUT THE INHERENT LAZINESS OF FORK TRUCK DRIVERS WAS NOT WELL RECEIVED IN THE WAREHOUSE.

"WE'VE GOT SOME GOOD NEWS AND SOME BAD NEWS, MR. STRICKLING. THE GOOD NEWS IS WE GOT RID OF THAT SQUEAK FOR YOU."

"THE COFFEE MAKER IS BROKEN."

AS THE ONLY EMPLOYEES IN THE OFFICE WHO DIDN'T HAVE DAUGHTERS SELLING GIRL SCOUT COOKIES, RON AND GREG WERE HUNTED DOWN LIKE ANIMALS.

"WE NEED MORE TONER."

ENTRY-LEVEL OFFICE CUBICLES.

"I HATE IT WHEN IT'S OHLER'S TURN TO DRIVE."

"SORRY ABOUT THAT LITTLE POWER OUTAGE THERE. WE WERE INSTALLING AN ELECTRIC AIR FRESHENER IN THE MEN'S ROOM. HOPE WE DIDN'T MESS UP YER DATA OR WHATEVER YER DOIN' THERE."

THE NEW CONVERGING CONFERENCE ROOM WALLS HELPED TO KEEP MEETINGS SHORT AND TO THE POINT.

"IN APPRECIATION FOR HIS SUGGESTION, WHICH WILL SAVE THE COMPANY MORE THAN $350,000 ANNUALLY, I AM PLEASED TO PRESENT AL WIMBOT WITH THIS EXQUISITE TIRE GAUGE, ENGRAVED WITH THE COMPANY'S LOGO!"

"JEEPERS! IS IT 12:25 ALREADY? A HALF HOUR JUST ISN'T ENOUGH TIME FOR LUNCH, IS IT?"

BASED UPON THE COMPUTER CALCULATIONS HE HAD RUN, LOWELL NEEDED TO HIT THE CEILING AT AN ANGLE OF 37° IN ORDER TO LAND HIS RUBBER BAND IN MILT'S COFFEE.

"MAINTENANCE SAYS THEY'LL BE HERE FIRST THING TOMORROW. THEY'RE TIED UP FIXING A LEAKY TOILET OVER IN PERSONNEL."

"HOW'S THAT HEAD COLD DOING, NOREEN?"

THE COMPANY PICNIC WAS YET ANOTHER EXAMPLE OF WADE'S INABILITY TO UNWIND.

KNOWING THAT HE WAS ABOUT TO BE FIRED, VERN TOOK
THE COMPANY CAR OUT FOR ONE LAST SPIN.

EMPLOYEES AT BURNFARB ASSOCIATES HAVEN'T QUITE
MASTERED THE FINE ART OF TRANSFERRING PHONE CALLS.

THE DRIVE-THRU WORKER'S NIGHTMARE.

"FOR HER 12 YEARS OF SERVICE AS A DATA PROCESSOR AND FOR KEYPUNCHING IN MORE THAN 3,789 RECORDS IN ONE EIGHT-HOUR SHIFT, PLEASE WELCOME OUR EMPLOYEE OF THE YEAR, MARGARET NEAL!"

"SO, HERE'S THE SITUATION, WARREN. EITHER I GET MY EIGHT PERCENT RAISE OR I'LL HAVE THIS SLIDE OF YOU AT THE COMPANY PICNIC BLOWN UP AND MAILED TO EVERY MEMBER OF THE BOARD OF TRUSTEES."

"HELEN, I KNOW WE'RE ON VACATION! I JUST NEED TO GET CAUGHT UP ON A LITTLE WORK! LIGHTEN UP!"

CRASH!

THUNK!

ALTHOUGH THEY RESPECTED HIS DEDICATION, THE OTHERS IN CHUCK'S CAR POOL REMINDED HIM THAT IT WAS 6:49 AND PERHAPS HE SHOULD START THINKING ABOUT DRIVING THEM ALL HOME.

AFTER MONTHS OF PLANNING, MANAGEMENT REVEALS THE NEW REORGANIZATION PLAN.

"ALL I DID WAS HIT THE DELETE BUTTON!!"

IT'S NEVER HARD TO SPOT THE SPOUSES AT THE ANNUAL OFFICE CHRISTMAS PARTY.

NORM PITLOFF WOULD GO TO ANY LENGTH TO USE THE HIGH-OCCUPANCY VEHICLE LANE.

"WHEEZE OR SOMETHING. I THINK YOUR BOSS IS CHECKING UP ON YOU."

"BY ADDING A NEW 120 MEGABYTE HARD DRIVE AND USING THE SOFTWARE THAT RICK DEVELOPED OVER THE LAST SIX MONTHS, WE CAN COMPUTE ANYBODY'S HANDICAP TO WITHIN 1/1000TH OF A STROKE."

TED FELT IT WAS IMPORTANT TO HAVE A RESUMÉ THAT WOULD CATCH THE PERSONNEL MANAGER'S EYE.

McPHERSON

SHORTLY AFTER LLOYD WAS KNOCKED UNCONSCIOUS, MANAGEMENT PUT AN END TO THE LUNCH HOUR JOUSTING MATCHES.

"HERE'S HOW IT WORKS: IF THE BALL HITS THE FLOOR IN YOUR CUBICLE, YOU'VE GOTTA BE ON CALL FOR THE WEEKEND."

"OH, BROTHER! HE'S BRINGING THE OVERTIME SHEET AROUND AGAIN!"

THE DOWNSIDE OF GOING ON A TWO-WEEK VACATION.

WILLARD MULNIK INADVERTENTLY FAXES HIS TIE TO
THE OMAHA OFFICE.

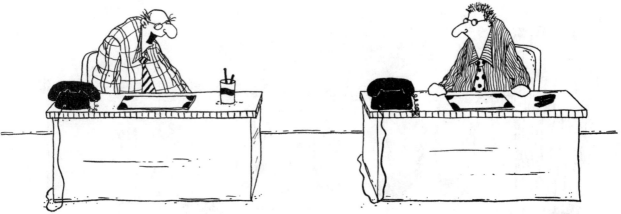

"I ARRANGED MY FLEX TIME SO THAT I'LL WORK FOURTEEN HOURS A DAY, SIX DAYS A WEEK AND THEN GET 1998 OFF."

ALTHOUGH CONVENIENT, HAVING YOUR DESK NEAR THE COFFEE MAKER HAS SOME DEFINITE DRAWBACKS.

"ART, THE SPILLMAN KID IS HERE. HE WANTS TO KNOW IF WE OFFER ANY KIND OF HEALTH PLAN IN ADDITION TO THE FIVE BUCKS WE'RE PAYING HIM TO MOW THE LAWN."

OUR REGIONAL MANAGERS THROUGH THE YEARS

S. ROBB
AUG 1988 – FEB 1989

M. OHLER
MAR 1989 – MAY 1989

J. SCHAAD
JUNE 1989 – JAN 1990

P. FRAWLEY
FEB 1990 – AUG 1990

B. WATKINS
OCT 1990 – NOV 1990

G. BECK
DEC 1990 – FEB 1991

C. L...
MAR 19...

P. CLARK
JULY 1991 – JUN 1992

NEWLY HIRED REGIONAL MANAGER VERN FEGMAN WAS STARTING TO WONDER WHAT HE'D GOTTEN HIMSELF INTO.

"IT'S FROM YOUR BOSS. IT SAYS, 'BEST WISHES FOR A SPEEDY RECOVERY'."

SECURITY HAD BEGUN TO CRACK DOWN ON PEOPLE LEAVING
THE PLANT WITH COMPANY PROPERTY

THE BOARD MEMBERS KNEW THE IMPORTANCE OF UNWINDING AFTER A HIGH-PRESSURED MEETING.

"THE COMPUTER SYSTEM IS DOWN AGAIN."

MORALE AMONG THE LITMAN INDUSTRIES SALES FORCE WAS DECLINING IN DIRECT PROPORTION TO THE COMPANY'S CUTS IN THE TRAVEL BUDGET.

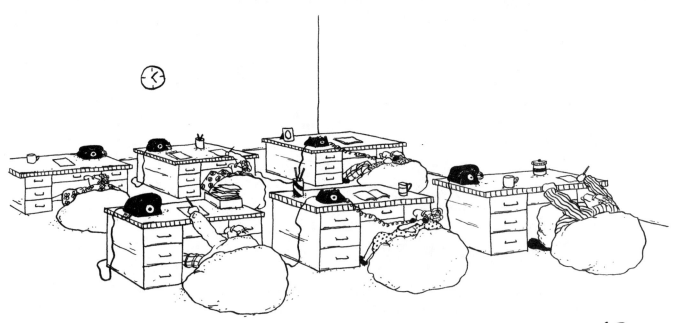

WORKING FOR THE NUMBER-ONE MANUFACTURER OF BEAN BAG CHAIRS DOES HAVE ITS DOWNSIDE.

ONE OF THE HAZARDS OF WEARING A BEEPER.

"NORM JUST GOT HIS LUMP SUM RETIREMENT FUND. HE WANTED IT ALL IN ONES."

LLOYD FINSTER WAS HAVING A TOUGH TIME ADJUSTING TO LIFE AS A RETIREE.